EMMANUEL FRICERO

THE RUSSIAN ORTHODOX CATHEDRAL
OF ST. NICHOLAS
IN NICE

BONECHI

© Copyright 1994 by CASA EDITRICE BONECHI s.r.l.
Via dei Cairoli 18/b - 50131 Florence (Italy)
Telex 571323 CEB - Fax 55/5000766

The proceeds of the sale of this book
are assigned exclusively to charity
purposes of the Orthodox Russian Church
Association, Nice, France.

ISBN 88-7009-410-3

THE CONSTRUCTION OF THE CATHEDRAL

The Russian Orthodox Cathedral of Nice is, without doubt, the most beautiful building of that faith outside of Russia and perfectly represents Russian art abroad.

Each year the cathedral welcomes thousands of visitors and tourists, many of whom enjoy attending the religious ceremonies celebrated on its premises.

Although their culture, religion, and artistic backgrounds differ, these visitors are unanimous in praising the beauty of the building, and the piety inspired by its interior, and they are infused by the mysticism and the splendor of the orthodox services.

This brochure is written for such visitors. Its purpose is to inform them why the city of Nice was selected for the raising of the cathedral and to give a few specifics as to its architectural style, icons and artistic wealth in general.

its mild climate would help her fragile health.

She was accompanied by several members of her family and a numerous entourage.

Many Russian families also followed her example and spent the winter months in Nice. Other foreign families imitated them, and thus this little Italian town of some 40,000 people with no railroad connection but with handsome and spacious villas (1) surrounded by magnificent parks, became a central point of attraction to an elegant and wealthy society.

During the same period, the bay of Villefranche became a Russian naval base following a treaty signed by Victor Emmanuel II, King of Sardinia. Many Russian naval officers and sailors either travelled through or stayed there for a period of time.

The Russian Colony before 1860 in Nice - Its spiritual needs - The building of the first orthodox church on rue Longchamp in 1859

From 1856 to 1860, the Empress Alexandra Feodorovna, widow of Emperor Nicholas I, stayed twice in Nice for some time*, hoping that

The former Russian Church in Nice (1860). A view of the "iconostas" (in carved oakwood).

(1) The term "villa" had a slightly different connotation in those days. It meant a cluster of several luxurious and large houses surrounded by a vast park.

Commemorative plaque: "This cathedral was edified owing to the solicitude and generosity of H.M. the Emperor Nicholas II and of his Royal Mother, the Dowager Empress Marie. Inaugurated on December 17, 1912.

Outside view of the Cathedral.

For services or other religious celebrations such as marriages, one had to travel to Marseilles where there was a Greek orthodox church, and such a trip in those days was only possible either by sea or horse-drawn carriage.

In 1857 during the first stay of Empress Alexandra Feodorovna and under her sponsorship and with her generous support, the building of a church on rue Longchamp was implemented. It was inaugurated in 1859. For more than fifty years it was the spiritual centre, not only for orthodox Russians, but also for all Christians in the region of the same faith: Greeks, Serbians, Rumanians, Bulgarians and others. Services are celebrated there regularly up to this day.

Its iconostas (the ornamented wall shielding the altar), holy pictures, and ornaments of the period are worth a visit. They are the work of M. N. Wassilieff, a professor of the Fine Arts Academy of Saint Petersburg, and were made in Russia.

The increase in the Russian colony - The active support of Empress Marie Feodorovna - The formation of a committee for the construction of a new church

During the second half of the last century, the population of Nice, now a French city, had more than trebled. It was serviced by railroads which linked it to Marseilles and to Genoa.

The Russian colony similarly increased. Many of its members had acquired estates and resided

The Russian colony grew in number. However, there was no Orthodox church in Nice. For rituals such as baptisms or last rites, the chaplains of the Russian navy in Villefranche had to be called in.

there all year. The church on rue Longchamp was clearly insufficient. The orthodox Russians, so attached to their religion and to the expression of their spiritual life, were worried by this situation. First, the question was raised regarding construction of a chapel in Villefranche, which was then a Russian naval base. The idea was given up because it would have been difficult for the Russians living in Nice to reach it, and also because the ships of the Russian navy had their chapels and their chaplains aboard. When they were away at sea, the number of Russians in

His Imperial Majesty Nicholas II.

Her Majesty the Dowager Empress Marie Feodorovna.

Villefranche was quite reduced.

The possibility of rearranging and enlarging the church on rue Longchamp was considered. However, the area of ground was too small to significantly increase the space set aside for the faithful, even if the existing church had been demolished in order to construct a new one.

Unforeseen circumstances finally put an end to these hesitations and concerns.

In 1896, Empress Marie Feodorovna, widow of Emperor Alexander III (2), came to spend the winter on the Riviera, at Cap d'Ail. She was attracted there by the presence in Nice of her sister, the Princess of Wales, who was staying at Mont Boron with her mother-in-law, Queen Victoria.

The Empress was accompanied by her two younger sons, Georges and Michael and her youngest daughter, the Grand Duchess Olga. She hoped that the mildness of the climate would be beneficial to the health of Prince Georges, then 25, and gravely ill with tuberculosis.

The Russian Orthodox parish of Nice was then served by archpriest Serge Lubimoff. He went frequently to Cap d'Ail, as chaplain to the Empress and her family. He thus had frequent opportunities to inform her of the spiritual needs and concerns of the Russian colony in Nice and of their desire to have a new church built.

The Empress was immediately attracted to this idea. Was it not in Nice that thirty years earlier she had the sadness of seeing her fiancé, Crown Grand Duke Nicholas Alexandrovitch die? Was it not there that her destiny was determined in that she married Emperor Alexander III?

Returning to Saint Petersburg, she acquired the necessary support, particularly that of her son, Emperor Nicholas II, and in 1900 she agreed to give her high sponsorship to the Committee to build a new Russian orthodox church in Nice. The presidency of this committee was given to Prince George Romanovsky, Duke of Leuchtenberg (3).

(2) Empress Marie Feodorovna was born Princess of Denmark. She was the younger sister of Alexandra, then Princess of Wales, and later queen of England. One of her brothers was George I, King of Greece, another one married a Princess of Bourbon-Orléans.

(3) Prince George Maximilianovitch Romanovsky, Duke of Leuchtenberg, was the grandson of Eugène de Beauharnais, and was installed at the Congress of Vienna, as Duke of Leuchtenberg. Through his mother he was the grandson of Emperor Nicholas I.

The first steps - Professor Preobrajensky's project - Its general characteristics - Its approval

The first concerns of the Committee were to raise funds and to look for ground suitable for the proposed goal. Toward the end of 1901, ground large enough was purchased, situated in a beautiful quarter of Nice, peaceful and far from the commercial center, at the intersection of rue Verdi and rue de Rivoli and rue Berlioz.

The study and development of the plans were entrusted to Professor Preobrajensky, professor of architecture at the Imperial Academy of Fine Arts in St Petersburg.

He had given proof of his architectural talent, notably by constructing the Cathedral of Reval and the Russian orthodox church in Florence which had been recently completed.

The choice of style, its concept, its layout, the establishment of overview plans and the rapid development of details and exterior ornamenta-tion of the building resulted in an admirable prototype of Russian religious architecture being achieved. Its author gave proof of great talent, perfect taste, and great competence.

In complete agreement with the desire of the imperial sponsor, and also without doubt influenced by the movement which was develop-ing at that time toward a return to national origins, as much in architecture as in all other forms of art, Professor Preobrajensky developed with remarkable talent the plan of a cathedral in the old Russian style of the churches of Moscow and Iaroslav of the time before Peter the Great (end of the XVIth century and the beginning of the XVIIth century).

Conforming to this style, the central cupola, which is the most important and the highest, is surrounded by four other majestic cupolas forming a harmonious ensemble of line and proportion characteristic of the religious architec-ture of that period. Of equal purity of line, but

Archpriest Serge Lubimoff, the first officiating priest of the Cathedral.

Prince Serge Galitzine, last president of the commission.

even richer in ornamental detail are the belfry and the two entry porches.

Let us note that it was the plot of ground selected in the first place at the intersection of two equally important streets which gave the architect the idea of constructing two entry porches of similar importance and aspect, one on each of the streets. The vast extent of the park where the church was finally built permitted retention of this plot which was favourable to the architectural aspect.

The construction borrowed heavily in its details from the cathedral of St Basil the Blessed in Moscow. The talent of Professor Preobrajensky consisted of harmoniously blending details into the total architecture of the new church. It is thus happily distinguished from the Moscow cathedral in which an overly gross relationship of details of styles and different periods can at times be shocking, rich as they may be.

On the other hand, the intuition and artistic sense of the architect permitted him to take into account the fact that the building would be set off against the rich background of the lively and brilliant colours of the sky and the Mediterranean atmosphere, so different from the hues of the sky in the North of Russia.

That is why in choosing the colours and tints of the building material, he did not slavishly imitate the material used in Russia and preferred dark and subdued colours, clear and luminous hues better in harmony with the natural environment: light brown for the exterior brick work, turquoise blue for the majolicas, and light grey for the stones. The architect personally studied even the least details of the exterior finish of the building and designed them in the purest style of XVIth and XVIIth centuries.

The project submitted by Professor Preobrajensky was remarkable and gave proof of rare talent. As soon as it was finished, he presented it to Empress Marie Feodorovna and to the members of the Committee and received their full approval. It was then submitted to the scrutiny and criticism of the technical Committee of the Saint Synode. It was approved without reserve. The only thing remaining was to execute it.

The period of difficulties - The choice of the ground - Park Bermond, the magnanimous gift of Emperor Nicholas II

An architect from Nice was put in charge to estimate the cost of the construction based on the cost of material and local labour and to oversee the execution of the work. Unfortunately, the nature of the underlying ground acquired on rue Verdi had been overlooked, and there was no assurance that it was capable of bearing the weight of a construction as heavy as that of a church as monumental as that foreseen.

After the foundations were dug, it was discovered that the quality of the soil was so poor that continuing construction would involve such difficult work that it would absorb most of the funds foreseen for the total construction.

After a few fruitless attempts, it was necessary to stop the work undertaken without any hope of restarting it. Neither funds nor usable ground were available. Discouragement spread among the members of the Committee.

This situation remained unclear for a number of months until the middle of 1902, when an event occurred which decided the site of the future cathedral in an ideal and unexpected way.

Emperor Nicholas II consented that the new church be built in Bermond Park, which was his personal property and which was located in one of the districts of Nice considered to have the best future. This authorization was due to the intervention of the dowager empress.

Probably it was not completely due to chance, but to a deeper reason, linked to a distant and sad past, and events which had occurred many years earlier in the same area and which had decided the destiny of the Empress Marie Feodorovna herself.

It was indeed, as stated above, in one of the residences of the Villa Bermond that the young Crown Prince Nicholas of Russia had died in 1865. His father Emperor Alexander II, had acquired Bermond Park soon after the death of his older son. His younger son, Emperor Alexander III, a friend and ally of France, inherited it in 1881. On his death, the estate passed in 1894 to Emperor Nicholas II (4). It was he who graciously donated Bermond Park to the Committee so that they could construct the new church.

This beautiful and vast park neighbored on larger roads, one of which bore the name of boulevard Tsarevitch.

Implementation of the project Laying the cornerstone - Problems to resolve

It was now a question of implementing the project and the plans of the architect, Mr. Preobrajensky: of making concrete his artistic concepts, of giving them life, and of making them a reality.

(4) It is well known that Emperor Nicholas II died as a consequence of his fidelity to the Allies. He was atrociously murdered in July 1918 in a basement in Ekaterinenburg with the Empress Alexandra, his four young daughters aged from 17 to 22, his son Alexis, a disabled child of 14, and a few loyal servants.

The patron saints of the Emperor Alexander II and of the members of his family.

But where could the necessary funds be found? How could respect for the style and perfection in its execution be assured with teams of workers who had never completed or even seen work of this type? The difficulty was even greater in that the project was of extreme complexity and the plans were the work of a Russian architect who was prevented by distance from directing works on the site.

It was to the construction committee that the problem of vanquishing these difficulties fell. It was they who had the honour of overcoming them.

Some preparatory work started, in order to provide easy access to the ground, and on 12 (25) April, 1903, (5) the anniversary of the death in Nice of the Crown Prince, the ceremony of laying the cornerstone of the building solemnly took place.

The weather was radiant. Numerous members of the Imperial Russian family who were staying at that time in the South of France, representatives of the French authorities, members of the orthodox clergy who had come from neighbouring towns, representatives of Russian, French, and foreign society were all present at the ceremony, surrounded by a large crowd. To cite some of those who took part: Grand Duke Michel Nicholaievitch, one of his sons Michel and his daughter Anastasia, the Duchess of Mecklembourg-Schwerin; the Duchess of Edinburgh; Duke Georges of Leuchtenberg; and Prince Ferdinand of Bulgaria. (6)

Then the daily work began little by little, inevitably including all kinds of difficulties which could be overcome only by the unflagging energy and inextinguishable will of members of the Committee all directed toward a single goal: final completion of the project.

Construction stretched out for more than nine years with several interruptions. Three presidents succeeded to the head of the Committee: His Imperial Highness Duke Georges of Leuchtenberg; A. I. Nelidoff, Russian ambassador to Paris; and Prince Serge Galitzine. Four architects from Nice were successively employed in overseeing the execution of the work and ensuring its conformity with the plans of the architect. Many times it was necessary to change technical personnel, contractors and suppliers.

A scrupulous respect for all small details of the plans of Professor Preobrajensky was the constant preoccupation of the Committee and the author of the project himself. The same care prevailed in meeting both architectural requirements and local climatic conditions. Their quality was precisely and meticulously defined in the contracts with the suppliers. Constant and difficult technical controls were ensured through help from experts and specialists, and by trial and error experiments in public and private laboratories, both on site and in Paris. Thanks to such controls, certain faults and defects were foreseen and avoided which would have been the cause of serious failings if had they been perceived too late. Without doubt, some of them would have been irreparable.

Financial difficulties - Interruption of the work - New providential intervention by the Emperor - End of the basic work

To the difficulties briefly enumerated above were added others of a purely financial nature. The rhythm of work had to be slowed and then in 1906, completely stopped, because of the lack of sufficient funds.

More than 500,000 gold francs had already been spent, an amount equivalent to more than 100 million francs currently (7), and moreover they were far from completing all the work as foreseen in the estimate.

Under these difficult conditions, the Committee had to spend all its activity and energy in seeking new funds. But the sums that they received, although important, were far from being sufficient to complete the work.

This disturbing situation which seemed without solution, lasted approximately two years, and one can wonder what would have happened if during the year 1908, an unexpected and providential event which completely changed the situation, had not occurred.

(5) The Julian calendar is behind the Gregorian calendar by thirteen days, whereby April 12, according to the Eastern Church, is the same as April 25 in the Julian calendar.

(6) Grand Duke Michael Nicholaievitch was the youngest son of Emperor Nicholas I. His son, Michael Mikhailovitch, also lived on the Côte d'Azur.
The Grand Duchess Anastasia had married, in 1879, the duke of Mecklembourg-Schwerin. She was the mother-in-law of Christian X of Denmark, of Crown Prince William of Prussia, and of Alexandra of Great Britain.
The Duchess of Edinburgh was the daughter of Emperor Alexander II.

(7) We calculate, here and later, that one gold franc before 1914 was worth 200 francs at the end of 1958 which is probably a little less than actual value.

The patron saints of the Emperor Nicholas II and of the members of his family.

Emperor Nicholas II wished to have the work restarted immediately and finished. At his request, Professor Preobrajensky was given the duty of establishing a very detailed and descriptive estimate of the work which remained to be done in order to ensure completion of the exterior building and to execute all the coverings and external decorations excluding, however, all the finishing details and ornamentation of the interior of the church. This estimate reached the amount of 700,000 gold francs (8). The Emperor, with his customary generosity, authorized this amount to be taken from the funds of his private chancery.

The Committee for overseeing the conduct of the work was reorganized under the effective presidency of Prince Serge Galitzine, a high functionary of the ministry of the imperial court and under the High Patronage of His Majesty the Emperor himself.

After a long interruption of almost two years, work started again at a fast pace. The five cupolas surmounting the cathedral were promptly built. They were made of reinforced concrete, a new process in construction which was then a novelty in building technique. Then the steeple and its cupola were built.

The main structure of the building was successfully finished.

(8) Or about 150 million francs of paper money 1958.

The Virgin Mary, Comforter of the Afflicted, surrounded by those who implored Her aid. ▶

THE DECORATION OF THE CATHEDRAL

The external decoration - The brick covering - Limestone and marble work - The majolicas and the tiles

There remained to accomplish the covering and external decorations of the building. It was a difficult task. It was necessary to strictly respect in all details the plans and drawings of the author of the project, Professor Preobrajensky. The diversity and delicacy of the rich ornamentation and the complexity of the plans necessitated material of a special nature and quality and highly skilled labour. The ragion scarcely had resources of these kinds. Thus, for example, the covering bricks of the outside had to be of exceptional quality. Their size had to be very exact and regular. Their light brown colour could not fade or darken under the influence of local atmospheric conditions and long sunny periods. Experiments were made on samples from different French, Russian, and German factories. Only the product of a factory in the Rhine region met the required conditions. The Rhenish bricks then were used for the external covering of the whole building including both entry porches and the bell tower.

Other, even much more difficult, tasks awaited the members of the Committee. It was necessary to be concerned with the furnishings and with the size and sculpture of the stones and marbles which were so important in the building. When one closely examines the blocks and slabs and the fine lace of the carved stones in the porches, the lightness and delicacy of the designs of the elements in stone and marble which abundantly adorn the whole building, from the bottom to the top, one realizes how much work and considerable expense were involved in this part of the project.

Almost all the stones used in the work came from limestone quarries and have a uniformly light grey colour and great hardness. The stone cutting and carving were entrusted to teams of specially well-qualified workers brought from Italy. They showed themselves to be masters in the difficult art of transforming stone of great hardness into a fine detail. The cost of this work grew to 465,000 gold francs, an enormous sum for the period (9).

The beautiful pastel blue color of the decorative majolicas, the design and the hue of tiles covering the cupolas, the bell tower and the entry porches

(9) Approximately 100 million paper francs money as of the end of 1958.

were specified by the architect after careful study. They were ordered partially from Florence, partially from Blois. Their cost reached 50,000 gold francs (10).

Thanks to the strict adherence to the plans and the technical specifications, the general exterior aspect of the cathedral presented the very satisfactory appearance that had been conceived and desired by Professor Preobrajensky: an assertive style, perfect harmony of colours and great lightness.

The entry porches - The bell tower - The cupolas - The mosaics

The execution of the external architecture of the bell tower and of the entry porches was the most difficult to realize. Decorative riches were accumulated there. The cupola of the bell tower is covered with genuine gold leaf. Its bays are sumptuously framed by finely sculpted marble and majolicas. Each of them, considered separately, constitutes a complete artistic ensemble. The general appearance of the bell tower is even more enriched by small balconies of white sculpted marble.

Each of the two entry porches constitutes a perfectly harmonious ensemble. Their very pure style is without exception sustained in every detail. The richness of the sculpted marble, of the pendentives, the design and the colour of the majolicas, the monumental columns of select limestone, everything is striking and captures the attention of visitors. The pyramids of the top are adorned by coloured tiles separated by six gold threads; they are crowned by two headed eagles, symbolic coat of arms of Russia of that period.

One is carried in thought to Moscow, to the cathedral of Saint Basil or to the Kremlin of former days.

The framings in sculpted marble of the great entry gates and the bays of the Southern fa ade were executed by Italian workers chosen from among the best. One does not truly know, before the perfection of these works of art, what is more admirable: the beauty of the designs created by the architect or the talent of the workers who executed them. They seem to have competed in achieving an admirable and perfect work of this type.

The six crosses with gold leaves above the cupolas were executed at Pistoia, in Tuscany following the designs of Professor Preobrajensky in the same style as the entire building (11). The solemn ceremony which, among Orthodox Christians, accompanies the erection of the first cross, took place on January 13, 1910, fiftieth anniversary of the inauguration of the first Russian church on rue Longchamp.

In order to enrich still more the external aspect of the building, its façades were adorned with mosaic icons. (12) They were executed by the great specialist Froloff, according to the sketches of the painter Vassilieff.

The Western façade is adorned with a large mosaic representing the Holy Face of the Saviour, surrounded by an embossed guilded copper canopy, and by majolicas. On the faces of each of the entry porches, one can see between the arch and the pendentives of sculpted marble, the mosaic icons of Saint Alexander Nevsky and of Saint Mary-Magdalena, the first as a memory to Alexander III, the second because it was the name of the dowager empress who had given, ten years earlier, her high patronage to the Committee for construction of the church.

Alcoves richly framed in marble are prepared to receive several other mosaic icons. The faithful who frequent or visit the cathedral do not doubt that someday in the near future, icons will come to complete the ornamentation of the façades.

The general appearance of the building - The clearing of its accesses - Avenue Nicholas II - Cost of the construction - Origin of the funds spent

In completing here the description of the exterior appearance of the cathedral, one should note once more to what extent it is enhanced by the place it occupies in the middle of the vast (10-acres) park and by the clear view one has of it from Boulevard Tsarevitch and other neighbouring streets as well. This very important question was deservedly the focus of the attention of the Committee. It was possible in 1911, to purchase the grounds which separated the park surrounding the church from Boulevard Tsarevitch.

The purchase included 2500 square meters, of which 500 were immediately donated to the City of Nice. The City created on it a large access road and the municipality gave to that road the name

(10) About 10 million paper francs as of the end of 1958.

(11) According to Russian tradition and custom, the faces of the crosses are oriented parallel to the wall on which the altar is placed.

(12) The word "icon" means holy image and applies to paintings on canvas, wood, or bronze as well as to mosaics or frescoes. The same name is given to modern images of all formats.

The Apostle Saint Peter and a few episodes from his life. ▶

of its donor, Avenue Emperor Nicholas II, which it bears to this day (13). The remainder of the ground on both sides of this avenue is still free of any building which would have impeded the view.

It was not always easy to protect these grounds from other uses which would have reduced the isolation of the cathedral. The grounds had great value, which increased with time. In the periods of financial difficulties, during the construction and afterwards, the sale of part of the land was considered for the construction of apartment houses. Mercifully, no irreparable act was committed. The financial difficulties were resolved in other ways, and the beautiful cathedral remains to this day visible from all points.

For the construction of the structure, the covering and the exterior decoration 1,500,000 gold francs were spent (14). In round numbers, the origin of this amount is as follows: His Majesty Emperor Nicholas II contributed 700,000 gold francs (15), not taking into account the gift of Bermond Park; Prince Serge Galitzine, last president of the Committee, always generously opened his purse in difficult moments and his donation reached 400,000 gold francs, not including his other rich gifts; approximately 300,000 gold francs were contributed by donors who specified what their contribution was to be used for. The remainder came from a variety of donations, income from invested funds awaiting utilization, and smaller contributions of all kinds.

Interior work - The role of the artist Pianovsky - Maintaining the unity of style - The choice of models

The completion of work on the structure, the covering and the exterior decoration completely exhausted existing financial resources. It was only thanks of the large monetary contribution of Prince S. Galitzine and a few other generous donors, always bestowed without hesitation or delay, that a level of achievement could be almost reached, as it is today.

There still remained, however, all the interior work: to cover the walls with decorative frescoes and sacred paintings, build the altar and the iconostas, with its icons, execute the panelling and the flooring, hang the doors, finish the bell tower with its indispensable carillon, provide the clergy with vestments and necessary accessories in the exercise of the religious services: chandeliers, suspended lamps, censers, and reading-desks without mentioning sacred vases, chasubles, stoles and other things.

The accomplishment of all these tasks was faced with endless and unceasing difficulties. The style of the interior work necessarily could not clash with that of the building and its exterior decoration. The plans and the drawings could not be studied and perfected anywhere else but in Russia itself by Russian artists, specialists in religious art. Certain elements like the altar, and the iconostas, the accessories for the services and the majority of the icons, could only be realized in Russian workshops having specialized workers skilled in the execution of this kind of work, and having the tools and indispensable raw materials in hand.

At the beginning of 1909, the Committee concerned itself with these grave questions and particularly the iconostas, the principal piece of every orthodox church. The Committee addressed the director of the Stroganoff painting school in Moscow, Mr. Nicholas Globa, an authority in the field and well known for his perfect knowledge of old Russian styles, Mr. Globa highly recommended for this work one of his young students, L. Pianovsky, certifying that he possessed all the qualifications to rapidly complete an artistic assignment of such importance.

Entrusted with this flattering responsibility, the young artist began his task with a great professional conscientiousness, as well as with the fervour of youth. He left for Iaroslav, where he worked for several months in the old churches of the city and neighbouring regions, celebrated for the purity of their style, the beauty of their frescoes, icons and interior ornamentation. Having scrupulously studied with attention all the details, he made numerous sketches of all the elements which seemed to him most appropriate for the building project in Nice. He furthered his study in the churches of Moscow, particularly in the Cathedral of the Assumption, in the Kremlin, and in that of Saint Basil the Blessed.

This important preparatory work permitted the painter Pianovsky to develop outlines for the two iconostas projects which he submitted to the Committee.

(13) Resolution of the municipal council on November 7, 1911.

(14) Or more than 300 million of paper money as of the end of 1958.

(15) About 140 million in francs as of the end of 1958.

The Archangel Saint Gabriel.

Saint Nicholas the Miracle Worker.

One of them was accepted unanimously. That is the one which was built and which can be admired in the Cathedral of Nice. It constitutes a synthesis of the most beautiful samples of religious art from the Moscow-Iaroslav school.

Thus, the royal gate (16) and the icon which crowns it are copies of those of the church of the Holy Prophet of Elie, in Iaroslav, which is a very old work.

One can cite models which have served as well for other elements of the iconostas.

The frescoes

The motives, the hues and the designs of the frescoes on the walls were borrowed by Pianovsky from the Saint John the Baptist church of the Tolchkova monastery, near Iaroslav. He was not, however, content with a simple copy. Having

been given the much greater dimensions of the cathedral of Nice, he put the drawings in proportion while emphasizing the lines and making the hues lighter, to better put them in harmony with the other decorative elements.

The plan foreseen was that the walls be decorated with large religious paintings. This intention could not be realized and, as a consequence, the decorative frescoes which were conceived to serve as a framework for the principal subjects, while enhancing their value, played a principal role for which they were not intended. As a result, their artistic value is, at times, underestimated, and ill founded judgements tend to be made of them.

(16) The royal door is in the center of the "iconostas" and leads directly to the altar. The two other doors of the iconostas like the royal gate have a very precise function consacrated by tradition and customs.

All the frescoes were due to the Italian artist Designori, following the sketches of L. Pianovsky. Generally speaking, Designori finished his task most satisfactorily, conscientiously and with talent. However, it is regrettable that for a long time he was forced to work alone, without receiving directions from the author of the sketches and without being able to ask for advice from a Russian artist more knowledgeable in work of this kind. As a result, a few mistakes were made for which it would be unjust to reproach him.

For instance, one can criticize the overly dark colour of the wide band which circles the walls, above the wood panelling. This colour does not agree with the light and clear tonality which is the dominant note of the decoration of the whole building.

On the other hand, it was noted that a few years later, the frescoes had deteriorated in several spots. It was feared that the pictorial ornamentation would disappear completely in time.

The experts consulted attributed this to the use of diluted colours of insufficient quality. In 1949 restoration was begun on the frescoes which had lost their original brightness. But this time, oil paints were used for the elements which had suffered the most and of which the design and the original colours were scarcely recognizable. They were restored scrupulously, one after another, and it was a great joy to note that the interior decoration of the cathedral had a new life, that the beauty of the decorative motives and, above all, that of the large, clear, and luminous surface which extended above the dark frieze below, had reappeared.

The "iconostas" and icons - The sanctuary and the holy altar

The principal piece of the interior decoration of the cathedral is without question the "iconostas" which, with the two big icons with which it is extended on both sides, constitutes an ensemble notable for its importance and beauty.

The ensemble is the work of the artist Pianovsky, with the collaboration of the renowned workshop of the Brothers Khliebnikoff in Moscow. The three parts of the iconostas, of embossed and chiselled metal, is a clever synthesis of the most beautiful models of religious art that can be found in older churches in Moscow, Iaroslav, Rostov-the-Great and others. Its execution required more than a year of work by experienced and skillful workers. Almost all the chiselling was done by hand. Just a few motives repeated frequently were duplicated mechanically. A few elements in beaten copper or in molten bronze are of a very fine workmanship as, for example, the cross, ornamented with chiselling, which dominates the iconostas. All the pieces in metal are covered with gold leaf.

The technical accomplishment is perfect in all points, and this result is due to the trusting and cordial collaboration between the author of the sketches with the supervisors and the workers.

The icons of the "iconostas" are executed in the spirit of the school of Simeon Ouchakoff, a famous painter of holy images of the second half of XVIIth century. He was the first to bring a certain realism to the classic work of the Byzantine school and to reduce its austerity which at times bordered on harshness. Almost all the paintings are by the painter Glazounoff.

The Holy Face of Our Lord Jesus Christ, at the right of the royal door, is the copy of a very old icon which is found in the Cathedral of the Assumption in Moscow. At the left of the same door, the icon of the Mother of Our Saviour is a very exact copy of a representation known as Our Lady of Korsoune, which adorns one of the halls of the episcopal palace of Rostov-the-Great in the administrative region of Iaroslav.

The two other local icons (17) are those of Saint Nicholas and Saint Alexandra. The first is a beautiful work of classical style. It represents Saint Nicholas the Miracle Worker, under whose patronage the cathedral is placed. The second is the image of the holy martyr Alexandra. One notes that the artist has represented, very curiously, this Roman empress dressed in a tunic ornamented with byzantine eagles.

The upper part of the iconostas includes a series of icons painted in the style of the Simeon Ouchakoff school.

In the center, above the royal door is a very beautiful image of Christ having at his sides His Most Holy Mother and Saint John the Baptist. It is a representation of the Holy Communion, the original of which is in the Saint Elie cathedral in Iaroslav.

One should also pay attention to the two icons which were placed in the cathedral only after the events of 1917. A group of Russian refugees who had found a temporary shelter in the South of France had the pious desire to perpetuate the memory of Emperor Alexander, the Liberator Tsar, and that of the martyr emperor, Nicholas II, to which the Cathedral of Nice owes its existence. Two great icons, of the same appearance and style, represent the Holy Patrons of the two emperors, their wives, and their seven and five

(17) The term "local icons" is a bad translation of "miestny ikony" which denotes icons which must, according to the use and tradition, embellish the "iconostas". They represent Christ, the Virgin Mary, and the Patron Saints of the church.

Our Lady of Korsoun.

The Sacred Face.

Following pages: iconostasis. ▶
General view.

children. They were painted by a Russian émigré painter with care and talent, and are placed on both sides of the iconostas from which they seen to extend.

The Holy Altar differs from those usually found, due to an original innovation.

There have been substituted in the heavy silk fabric, formerly always interwoven with gold and silk thread, motifs in relief of cast and chiselled bronze which depict, with much art, the Last Supper. It was executed in the workshops of the Brothers Khliebnikoff, in accordance with the sketches of Pianovsky. The heavy and massive chandeliers with seven branches in bronze were made in similar fashion.

The image of the Holy Trinity, painted in fresco on the eastern wall behind the altar and consequently little noticed by visitors, is due to the brush of the painter Wassilieff. In spite of the unquestionable talent of the artist, this work is in unfortunate contrast, in its tone and abrupt lines, with the general tonality of the church and particularly with that of the sanctuary (18).

(18) The sanctuary is that part of the choir situated behind the "iconostas". It is there that the Holy Altar is placed. It is only partially visible when the royal door is open.

Description of several other important icons

The two great icons in front of the higher part of the choir draw attention.

The one on the left represents the Holy Apostle Peter and some of the scenes from his earthly life. According to the wish of the donor, it is in memory of Pierre Stolypine, the reform minister, assassinated in 1911. The other represents Our Lady of the Seven Sorrows.

To the right of the choir, on a door currently locked, on the Southern fa ade is a great icon of the Crucifixion executed on canvas in the style of Victor Vasnetsoff school. It is a perfect example of the art of the master of Russian religious painting.

Facing it on the Northern wall is a great image of the Archangel Michael painted in pink and golden hues which symbolize the flaming reflection of his sword of fire.

It was a gift made on the occasion of the tricentenary of the Romanoff dynasty in 1913. In front of it is suspended a lamp of very fine work.

These latter two icons are the work of the artist Pianovsky, and were executed in his workshop in Russia, as were the icons of Our Lady of Korsoune and of the Blessed Saviour, for which he received high praise.

The icons are placed in very beautiful frames, adorned with chiselled and embossed metal. Beautiful lamps illuminate them.

Facing the "iconostas" at the end of the church, against the western wall, is a big icon painted on wood representing Saint Alexander Newsky. It was offered by Prince Romanovsky,

The Royal Door -
access to the Altar.

Duke of Leuchtenberg, in memory of the Tsar Liberator, Emperor Alexander II, killed by a bomb in March 1881 (19).

In the confessional on the left, looking towards the altar, is found a large and beautiful tableau in bronze of Saint Nicholas the Miracle Worker by an unknown, but talented artist. The Saint is represented standing, of normal height, in his sacerdotal vestments. The hues are clear and light and pastel. According to the tradition of the Russian religious iconography, the features of the Saint reflect piety, goodness and benevolence.

In the confessional on the right is a beautiful tableau of the Crucifixion. It is the copy of a work by the French painter Laserge which is found in the Sorbonne in Paris.

The icon of Saint Nicholas - Its edifying history - The Virgin of Kazan

An icon placed on a false reading desk to the left and facing the higher part of the choir and which represents Saint Nicholas the Miracle Worker, is of particular interest. It is a very old image, placed in a richly hand carved walnut frame.

It belonged to Crown Prince Nicholas Alexandrovitch, the oldest son of Emperor Alexander II: when he died in Nice in April 1865, the icon was at his death bed. A little later, his mother, the Empress Marie, donated it to the Russian church of rue Longchamp where the funeral of her son took place. Then, when the commemorative chapel was built at the spot where the young prince expired, the icon was hung over the entrance door. It stayed there for many years.

But one day it was seen that under the intense rays of the sun and because of the atmospheric conditions, many clear signs of deterioration were appearing. The varnish which covered the painting were gathering in darker drops. With time, the whole image took on an uniformly blackened colour under which neither the design nor the old colour could be distinguished any longer.

The icon was taken away and put near the altar, behind the "iconostas". It remained there for a long time in its unrecognizable condition.

Twenty years went by, and in May 1945, it was noticed that in spots, clear or lightly coloured traces were appearing. The process continued day by day, when by a miracle, it was again possible to see the line and the original colours; gradually,

(19) Emperor Alexander II was thus named when in 1861 he liberated the Russian peasants from serfdom and made them free men.

it took on the appearance which it has today. Expert consulted on the matter stated that it was impossible to explain scientifically such a renovation, and that it was not due to human intervention. They could only ascribe this to humanly inexplicable causes in the current state of our knowledge.

The believers saw thus, justly, in that renovation a miraculous intervention of Providence. The icon was transferred to the church, in front of the rood-screen. It is an object of veneration by the faithfuls.

Another icon is placed symetrically with the former one to the right of the choir: it represents Our Lady of Kazan. Painted on wood and placed like the preceding icon on a false reading desk, it

The Holy Altar.

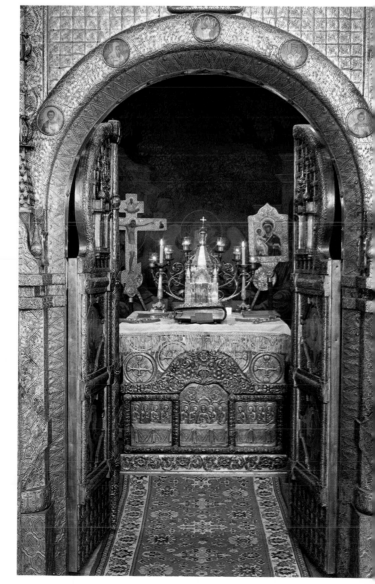

Our Lady of Kazan.

A few other remarkable works

Against the northern wall, at the foot of the rood-screen, a very particular and unique work can be admired. It attracts attention by its size, its richness and its perfect execution. It is a figurative representation of the Holy Sepulchre, made in the workshop of the Brothers Khliebnikoff previously mentioned.

The body of Our Lord lying, wrapped in the Holy Shroud, rests on the slab of the Sepulchre made of golden bronze and decorated with light blue enamels. Whatever opinions may be on the artistic value of this work, one must note its great richness, its care of perfect finish and the interest which it has of being, without doubt, the sole execution of this type.

There are in the cathedral a great number of small icons of very diversified artistic value. They have the advantage of permitting one to view the successive styles in Russian religious iconography, the differences which distinguish them, the traditions from which they took their qualities, and the religious spirit which inspires them.

Among religious cult accessories of pure Russian style, one is struck by four great candle-bearers placed before the big icon cases of the choir and by four suspended lamps in front of the "local icons" of the iconostas. They are copies of authentic pieces of the XVIIth century which are found in the Cathedral of the Assumption in Moscow. They were executed in the workshop of the Brothers Khliebnikoff and are due to the generosity of a group of parishioners.

As a conclusion to this summary description of the beautiful interior decoration of the cathedral, one has to bring out the most important role of the artist Pianovsky. Not only did he make the plans, draw the sketches after long visits to the most magnificent products of Russian religious art of the period chosen by Professor Preobrajensky, but he also oversaw the work in the workshops and with his skillful brush he himself painted many icons. One can say that for several years he dedicated body and soul to the task of which he had accepted the responsibility: one can find nothing in his work which is not in harmony with the ensemble of the building. That is the great talent of the artist to which all persons of recognized competence who have visited the cathedral after its completion have paid homage.

One should also note that almost everything which adorns the church: icons, carved wood, chiselled metal are gifts of pious people, generous and devoted to the church. We shall not cite their names. God knows them. We shall make an exception in favour of Prince Serge Galitzine, the last president of the Committee. Not only did he contribute a significant part to financing the

represents Our Lady of Kazan. It is framed and partially covered with chiselled and embossed silver, with a rich garnishing of pearls, precious stones, coloured stones and also jewels offered by the faithful in thanks for wishes granted, for recoveries or in simple devout homage. It was executed in the XVIIth century style by art workshop in Moscow.

A very beautiful banner, provided with a staff, on which are depicted the Virgin and Child, of woven and embroidered silk and with ornamented colour stones, is of the same origin.

The Holy Sepulchre.

construction, but he also took over all the expenses of the superb "iconostas".

An indispensable part of every Russian church are hanging bells in the bell tower. They are nine in number, of varied and well matched timbre, constituting a very complete carillon of perfect sonority. Eight of them were offered by the very generous sponsor whom we have already cited. The ninth, the heaviest, was cast in Marseilles and the order specified very exactly the tone desired. This single bell cost 5,000 gold francs, more than a million francs today.

Most of the decorative wood work was done in Parisian workshops after the drawings of Professor Preobrajensky. They are particularly remarkable for the perfection of their execution and their sculptures.

One could prolong this description and speak of the sacred vases and of the very rich collection of liturgical headdresses, chasubles and other sacred vestments which the cathedral possesses. This wealth is not a part of the church, and to describe these elements would be long and perhaps tedious for the visitor who cannot admire them, except on rare occasions. One day their description will complement this brochure.

Our Lady.

Icon of the Resurrection, surrounded by icons of the 12 principal Feast Days.

Dedication of the cathedral - The ceremony - The watchful presence of the French authorities

The solemn dedication took place on November 18, 1912. The Holy Synod of the Russian orthodox churches had bestowed on the church built in Nice, the title of cathedral. It was a unique event for a Russian church built outside of the Empire. The Russian church of rue Daru in Paris itself did not have such a title.

The weather was magnificent, and the bright colours of the building and its cupolas stood out with clarity against the pink and gold background of the sky.

The heavy gold crosses seemed to float in the transparent blue sky. The building appeared in all its splendour, shining with beauty, imposing in its majesty, and the subject of everyone's admiration.

Prince Alexander Romanovsky, Duke of Leuchtenberg, and the Grand Duchess Anastasia, daughter of the Grand Duke Michel, represented the imperial family. Prince Romanovsky wore crosswise the wide blue ribbon of the Order of Saint Andrew. General Goiran, commander of the army corps of the south eastern region, was in full uniform. He wore the red ribbon with yellow edging of the cross of Saint Anne of Russia.

Members of the Imperial Family, representatives of foreign courts, French authorities, including those from the municipality of Nice, and several members of the Russian colony filled the nave of the cathedral. A considerable crowd invaded the surrounding park and filled the windows, balconies and roofs of the neighbouring houses.

The ceremony of the dedication was celebrated by the deputy Bishop of Moscow, surrounded by many members of the clergy. All wore chasubles embroidered with gold and silver and sparkling mitres. The chants of a renowned choir from Moscow, resounded admirably in the very high nave (20).

According to the sacred rites, the Bishop headed the procession which walked round the cathedral. The gold and silver of the chasubles and the mitres were blazing in the sun. The ceremony was impressive because of its majesty, magnificence and richness.

Prince Galitzine, president of the Committee, and the archpriest Lubimoff who had dedicated for ten years their time and efforts to this labour, were honored. It was to the care of this holy priest whose name has not been forgotten in Nice, that the Bishop entrusted the cathedral.

The ceremony which started about 8 o'clock lasted for three hours. The Russian choir and the municipal orchestra directed by M. Solar, took their places in the park and performed Russian and French anthems and a cantata from the celebrated opera by Glinka, "A Life for the Tsar".

(20) The height of the dome is approximately fifty meters.

The Archangel Saint Michael.

Saint Alexander Nevsky (XIII century).

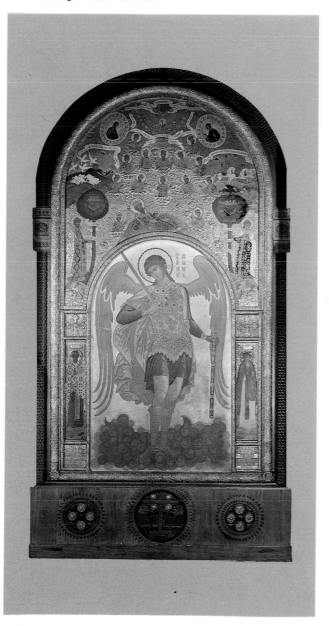

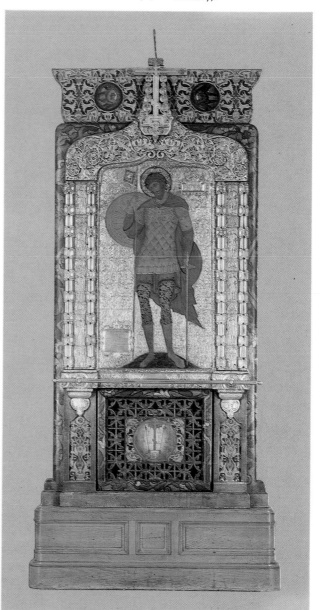

The inauguration of the Cathedral on December 17, 1912.

Conclusion - Predictions realized

And so this splendid House of the Lord started and came into being, as a place to pray for a life according to the teachings of Christ.

Many are those who during the ten years that the work lasted, dedicated themselves with complete selflessness to the goal. Two persons, however, Prince Galitzine and the archpriest Serge Lubimoff played a preponderant role. Their names remain linked with that of the Cathedral of Saint Nicholas for they were the acting force and, one can say, the soul of this accomplishment. They gave themselves without restraint, with all their might, all their spirit and consacrated to it all that which had been left to them in this world. They never doubted the future and when they did despair, one of them wrote:

"When the building is finished, and when in the magnificent park the imposing cupolas with their dazzling golden crosses are erected, when the solemn call of the bells resound, then together with orthodox Christians, many foreigners from other religions will come in great numbers to attend our religious services, and to enjoy with us our sacred hymns in honor of our Glorious God. Artists and friends of art will come to admire and to study the beauty of its so very Russian architecture. They will be able to get their inspiration without abandoning their western traditions".

This foresight was not only realized, but greatly exceeded. It is by tens of thousands that each year tourists from all countries and of all faiths and beliefs visit the Cathedral of Nice as a monument of rare beauty. They have before their eyes a splendid and beautiful church, of a new style for them, richly and harmoniously decorated and remarkable for its external architecture as well as for its interior ornamentation.

A few years after the inauguration in this sanctuary of ancient Russia, the most recent, the most impressive and the most beautiful, there gathered a crowd of unhappy people having lost in the storm which was sweeping the world what is closest to the heart of man: their land, their family, the physical and spiritual world in which they had always lived.

Here, in their exile, far from their country, they found the memory of the great past of their country (temporarily humiliated and reduced) and the possibility of praying to God as they formerly had in their native land, in a typically Russian church where everything speaks to the heart.

THE CHAPEL IN MEMORY OF THE TSAREVITCH NICHOLAS

A few years later, by the end of 1864, the Crown Prince of Russia, Nicholas Alexandrovitch, a handsome and charming young man of 20, came to Nice to try to recover from the grave illness with which he was afflicted. He settled in one of the residences of Villa Bermond (21). His mother, the Empress Marie Alexandrovna, settled in one of the residences of Villa Peillon, separated from the former by a simple fence.

However, it was too late. The doctors called to his bedside were powerless to help. The young Prince died on April 24, 1865, in the arms of his father, Emperor Alexander II, who had come from Saint Petersburg, and of his mother, and in the presence of many relations and friends and of his young and charming fiancée, Princess Dagmar of Denmark.

The funeral was celebrated among a grief-stricken crowd in the church of rue Longchamp, and the remains of the Prince were transported to Saint Petersburg, on a Russian ship, the frigate Alexander Nevsky (22).

Some time later, the Emperor privately acquired a portion of the vast park of the Villa Bermond.

(21) The residence where the Crown Prince died became the commemorative chapel. That occupied by the Empress became the private hospital Belvedere, boulevard Tsarevitch. All the other residences of both villas Bermond and Peillon have been demolished.

(22) Details of the stay in Nice, of the death and the funeral of the Hereditary Prince are in a brochure which can be purchased by visitors at the entrance of the cathedral.

The Chapel in memory of the Grand Duke Nicholas, son of Emperor Alexander II.

A beautiful commemorative chapel was built on the very spot where his eldest son had died. Consecrated in 1867, the chapel became a place of pilgrimage and was decorated with paintings, icons, and precious objects presented mostly by the regiments and military organizations of which the Prince had been the head. The icons were painted by the Russian artist K. Neff, very-well known at that time.

The pure byzantine style and the imposing appearance and interior of the Chapel decoration are worthy of the admiration of connoisseurs and artists. The Chapel itself perpetuates the memory of a young Prince whose premature death affected many.

It is interesting to note that the city of Nice gave a tangible proof of its sympathy with the events mourned by Russia, by naming a wide road near the chapel, Boulevard Tsarevitch.

General views of the Chapel.

CONTENTS